10 REASONS WHY TRADING IS THE BEST JOB

- Unlimited Potential For Success, Freedom, And Personal Growth

GODFX

Copyright © 2024 GODFX

All rights reserved

The characters and events portrayed in this book are fictitious. Any similarity to real persons, living or dead, is coincidental and not intended by the author.

No part of this book may be reproduced, or stored in a retrieval system, or transmitted in any form or by any means, electronic, mechanical, photocopying, recording, or otherwise, without express written permission of the publisher.

ISBN-13: 9798342410724
ISBN-10: 1477123456

Cover design by: Art Painter
Library of Congress Control Number: 2018675309
Printed in the United States of America

To all the determined traders who dare to break boundaries and chase the dream of financial freedom. May this book guide you through the challenges, ignite your passion, and empower you to build a future of wealth and purpose—not just for yourselves, but for the generations to come.

To the mentors and educators who generously share their wisdom, shaping the future of trading with their insights and support. Your commitment creates a legacy of success, ensuring the growth of the trading community and its lasting influence.

And to my family and friends, whose encouragement and belief have been my greatest strength. Your faith in me has fueled my ambition, and your love has given me the courage to pursue my dreams. This journey is ours together, and I am forever grateful.

"The journey of a trader is not just about wealth, but the mastery of self—where discipline meets opportunity, and freedom becomes a daily reality."
— GODFX

THIS BOOK IS DEDICATED TO EVERYONE WHO DREAMS OF BREAKING FREE FROM THE ORDINARY—MAY TRADING OPEN THE DOORS TO UNLIMITED POTENTIAL, FREEDOM, AND FULFILLMENT.

CONTENTS

Title Page

Copyright

Dedication

Epigraph

Foreword

Introduction

Preface

Prologue

Chapter 1: Introduction – Why Trading is the Ultimate Profession	1
Chapter 2: Unlimited Income Potential – Mastering the Markets for Financial Freedom	5
Chapter 3: Freedom & Flexibility – Designing a Life on Your Terms	10
Chapter 4: Independence – The Power of Self-Reliance in Trading	15
Chapter 5: Low Barriers to Entry – Opportunity for Everyone	20
Chapter 6: Constant Learning – Embracing the Lifelong Journey of Growth	26
Chapter 7: Personal Development – Building Resilience, Discipline, and Emotional Control	32
Chapter 8: Instant Feedback – Rapid Improvement and	37

Refining Your Strategy

Chapter 9: Global Markets & Liquidity – Tapping into Worldwide Opportunities	42
Chapter 10: Impactful Wealth Creation – Trading Beyond Financial Gains	47
Chapter 11: Legacy – Passing on Knowledge and Building a Future	51
Chapter 12: Conclusion – Your Journey Starts Now	55
Epilogue	57
Afterword	59
Afterword	61
Acknowledgement	63
About The Author	65
Praise For Author	67
Books In This Series	69
Books By This Author	73

FOREWORD

In a world that often values security over freedom and routine over independence, trading stands out as a bold and unconventional choice. For many, the allure of a steady paycheck, predictable hours, and a clear path of promotion feels safe—but for others, it feels stifling. Trading is the opposite of conventional. It offers no guarantees, no fixed schedules, and no limits. Instead, it offers something far greater: control over your life.

I remember when I first stumbled into the world of trading. Like many, I was drawn by the promise of financial success, but what I discovered was so much more. Trading didn't just offer a way to make money—it offered a way to redefine my life. It gave me the freedom to work from anywhere, the flexibility to design my own schedule, and the opportunity to grow not only financially, but personally. Trading became a path of self-mastery, discipline, and constant learning. Every trade, every market movement was a chance to improve, reflect, and evolve.

But let's be clear: trading is not a shortcut to success. It's not a lottery ticket. It's a craft, a profession, and, for many, a lifelong journey. It demands resilience, patience, and a commitment to growth. The challenges can be as profound as the rewards, but for those who stick with it, trading offers something that few other professions do—the chance to truly live on your own terms.

This book is a guide to why trading stands out as the ultimate profession. It's not just about the potential for wealth, but the broader benefits it brings—freedom, flexibility, and personal empowerment. Whether you're new to the world of trading or looking to deepen your understanding, these **10 reasons** will show you why trading is far more than just a job—it's a gateway to a life of independence and limitless possibilities.

As you read this book, I encourage you to keep an open mind and an open heart. Trading is a journey that requires both intellect and intuition, and it has the power to transform not only your financial situation but your entire approach to life. I hope this book inspires you to embrace the challenge and the rewards of trading, and to see for yourself why it's the best profession in the world.

Welcome to the adventure. Your journey starts here.

— GODFX

INTRODUCTION

In today's fast-paced, evolving world, traditional career paths no longer guarantee success or security. Many people spend years working in jobs that leave them unfulfilled, trapped in routines, and confined by the limitations of a fixed salary and rigid schedules. The dream of true financial freedom, personal independence, and the ability to live life on one's own terms seems elusive for most.

Enter trading—the profession that breaks all the traditional boundaries. It offers a unique combination of financial opportunity, flexibility, and personal growth. Trading, when approached with discipline and the right mindset, can be one of the most rewarding jobs in the world. It allows you to be your own boss, choose your own hours, and leverage global financial markets to build wealth in ways that many other professions simply cannot offer.

But make no mistake: trading isn't a "get rich quick" scheme. It requires patience, strategy, and the willingness to learn from both successes and failures. For those who are committed to mastering the craft, however, the rewards go far beyond financial gain. Trading sharpens your mind, builds resilience, and offers unparalleled freedom to shape your life in ways that resonate deeply with your goals and dreams.

In this book, we'll break down the **10 reasons why trading is the best job** you can have. We'll explore the limitless income potential, the independence it brings, the personal growth it fosters, and much more. Whether you're considering trading as a career or already on your journey, this guide will highlight what makes trading not just a profession, but a lifestyle of empowerment and limitless possibilities.

Get ready to see why trading stands above the rest as the ultimate path to success and fulfillment. Welcome to the world of trading—where your potential is truly in your hands.

— GODFX

PREFACE

In a world where the traditional 9-to-5 job often limits our potential, trading stands out as a profession that offers something rare—true freedom. Trading is not just a career; it's a lifestyle that empowers individuals to take control of their time, financial future, and personal development. With no boss dictating your schedule, no ceiling on your income, and the ability to work from virtually anywhere in the world, it's easy to see why so many are drawn to this path.

But trading is much more than the allure of freedom and wealth. It's a profession that demands discipline, constant learning, and emotional resilience. For those willing to put in the effort, trading offers a unique opportunity for personal and professional growth. The lessons learned in the markets are ones you can apply to every aspect of your life—building patience, cultivating mental toughness, and learning to make decisions with clarity and confidence.

In this book, we'll explore the **10 reasons why trading is the best job**. Whether you're a seasoned trader or just starting out, this guide is designed to inspire you, challenge you, and show you why trading can be the ultimate path to success, freedom, and fulfillment. It's not just about financial gain—it's about becoming the best version of yourself in the process.

Welcome to the world of trading, where the possibilities are limitless.

— GODFX

PROLOGUE

Imagine waking up in the morning knowing that your day is entirely yours to shape. There's no commute to battle, no boss to answer to, and no rigid schedule tying you down. Instead, you have access to the vast global markets—where the only limit to your success is your own knowledge, discipline, and determination.

This is the life of a trader.

Trading is not just about making money; it's about achieving freedom—financial freedom, personal freedom, and freedom over your time. It offers a pathway to build wealth without the constraints of traditional jobs, where the ceiling on your income is determined by someone else and where your time is rarely your own.

But trading is also a mirror. It reflects back your strengths, weaknesses, fears, and desires. It forces you to confront your emotions and grow in ways that few other professions do. The market is a place of constant learning, and in it, every decision you make provides instant feedback for improvement. Mastering trading is mastering yourself.

This journey is not for the faint of heart. It's challenging, unpredictable, and at times, unforgiving. But for those who embrace the challenge, trading offers something truly priceless: the ability to shape your own destiny.

This book is for those who are drawn to that challenge. Whether you're just starting out or already walking the path, these **10**

reasons why trading is the best job will inspire, motivate, and guide you. Trading may not be easy, but it's a journey worth taking—for the rewards are far greater than just financial gain. It's the path to ultimate freedom.

Welcome to the world of trading, where the possibilities are infinite, and the adventure is just beginning.

— GODFX

CHAPTER 1: INTRODUCTION – WHY TRADING IS THE ULTIMATE PROFESSION

Trading is frequently perceived as a gamble or a get-rich-quick scheme, but this could not be further from the truth. Those who dedicate themselves to mastering the art of trading discover that it offers unparalleled opportunities for financial freedom, flexibility, and personal development. Unlike many traditional professions, trading gives individuals the chance to control their own destiny—both financially and professionally. In this chapter, we'll dive into why trading is far more than just buying and selling; it's a life-altering path that can provide you with the ultimate freedom and independence.

Key Themes:

1. Overview of Trading's Unique Benefits
Trading stands apart from conventional careers in several

keyways:

Unlimited Income Potential: There are no ceilings in trading. Your earnings are directly tied to your performance and strategy. With the right skills, you have the power to scale your income infinitely, unlike salaried jobs where you're limited by a pay scale.

Complete Flexibility: Trading offers the freedom to work whenever and wherever you want. All you need is an internet connection. This flexibility means that you can design your life around your own priorities—be it family, travel, or hobbies—without sacrificing financial opportunities.

Independence and Control: As a trader, you answer to only yourself. You decide your own strategy, manage your own time, and control your financial future. This independence is rare in traditional jobs, which often come with strict hierarchies, teams, and processes.

Constant Personal Growth: Trading forces you to grow both technically and emotionally.

2. Comparison with Other Traditional Professions
Compared to traditional jobs, trading offers significant advantages:

No Salary Caps: In traditional professions, your income is usually limited by a fixed salary, with incremental raises often tied to promotions or years of experience. Trading, on the other hand, gives you the freedom to earn based on your skills and decisions.
No Office Politics or Corporate Structures: Corporate life often involves dealing with complex hierarchies, team dynamics, and office politics. Trading eliminates these barriers. You're free from bosses, coworkers, and company policies—making it a pure meritocracy.

Low Barrier to Entry: Many high-paying careers require years of education and large investments in degrees or certifications. While trading does require learning and practice, it doesn't demand the same level of financial investment or formal education to get started.

Immediate Feedback: In most jobs, it can take months or years to see the results of your work. Trading provides instant feedback—you know immediately whether your decision was profitable or not. This helps you refine your strategies and grow rapidly.

3. Introduction to the Upcoming Chapters and Topics
In the following chapters, we will break down the top 10 reasons why trading is the ultimate profession and how it can transform your life:

Unlimited Income Potential (Chapter 2) will explore how trading gives you the power to earn as much as your skill allows, with no income limits.

Freedom & Flexibility (Chapter 3) will dive into the ways trading allows you to design a life of freedom, from your location to your schedule.

Independence (Chapter 4) will highlight the benefits of self-reliance, where you call the shots and take control of your financial destiny.

Low Barriers to Entry (Chapter 5) will show you why trading is accessible to anyone willing to learn and invest in their growth.

Constant Learning (Chapter 6) will cover how trading keeps you engaged with a dynamic environment, ensuring that your growth never stagnates.

Personal Development (Chapter 7) will explore the internal qualities trading builds—resilience, emotional control, and discipline—that extend beyond the markets into your daily life.

Instant Feedback (Chapter 8) will discuss the rapid feedback loops that allow traders to improve and refine their strategies.

Global Markets & Liquidity (Chapter 9) will demonstrate the vast opportunities available across global markets, where traders can find liquidity and opportunities at any time.

Impactful Wealth Creation (Chapter 10) will show how trading can build generational wealth and positively impact your family and community.

Legacy (Chapter 11) will focus on how traders can pass on their knowledge and leave a legacy for future generations.

This chapter sets the foundation for understanding why trading is more than just a career—it's a gateway to independence, financial freedom, and a life built entirely on your terms. You'll get an overview of what makes trading unique, why it's a better option than most traditional careers, and a preview of the key benefits we'll explore in the rest of the book.

CHAPTER 2: UNLIMITED INCOME POTENTIAL – MASTERING THE MARKETS FOR FINANCIAL FREEDOM

One of the most powerful aspects of trading is the limitless income potential it offers. Unlike traditional careers where compensation is based on hourly wages or fixed salaries, trading allows your earnings to be tied directly to your skills, knowledge, and ability to capitalize on opportunities in the market. In this chapter, we explore why trading breaks the mold of conventional income structures, how skill development plays a crucial role in achieving financial freedom, and real-life examples of traders who have scaled their earnings to incredible heights.

Key Themes:

1. Why Income in Trading is Not Capped

In most traditional professions, income is limited by either the number of hours worked, or the position held within a company. A salaried employee may receive raises and bonuses, but these are generally incremental and capped. In contrast, trading offers a unique, uncapped earning potential because your income is directly tied to your performance and market opportunities. The more proficient you become in reading market trends, developing strategies, and executing trades, the greater your ability to generate profit.

Key Factors Contributing to Unlimited Income in Trading:

Performance-Based Earnings: In trading, there are no limits on how much you can earn. Your income is determined by your ability to identify profitable opportunities, manage risk, and execute trades with precision.

Scalability: As you accumulate experience and success in the markets, you can scale your operations by increasing the size of your trades, investing in more diverse markets, or utilizing leverage. This scalability allows traders to exponentially grow their earnings.

Global Market Access: The financial markets are vast, offering countless opportunities across various asset classes—forex, stocks, commodities, and cryptocurrencies. With access to global liquidity, traders have the potential to profit from an endless range of market conditions, whether bullish, bearish, or neutral.
This uncapped income potential means that traders are not limited by external factors like job titles, seniority, or working hours. Their financial success is entirely within their control, driven by their own performance and market understanding.

2. The Role of Skill Development in Achieving Financial Independence

While the prospect of limitless income is appealing, it's important to recognize that this potential can only be realized through constant skill development and discipline. Trading is a craft that must be mastered, and the journey to financial freedom involves acquiring the knowledge, experience, and mental resilience to navigate the markets effectively.

Key Areas of Skill Development:

Market Knowledge: Successful traders have a deep understanding of market dynamics, economic indicators, and price patterns. They stay updated on global news, geopolitical events, and financial data that can influence the markets. Continuous education and learning are vital to maintaining an edge.

Risk Management: To ensure long-term profitability, traders must develop a strong risk management system. This includes setting stop-loss orders, calculating position sizes, and managing exposure to avoid catastrophic losses. Mastering risk management is critical to preserving capital while pursuing higher gains.

Strategy and Analysis: Developing a well-thought-out trading strategy is essential to success. Traders use technical analysis, fundamental analysis, and quantitative models to make informed decisions. Over time, they refine their strategies based on what works best for their individual style, risk tolerance, and market conditions.

Emotional Discipline: Emotional control is a key factor in achieving financial independence through trading. Fear, greed, and impatience can sabotage even the most promising trades. Successful traders learn to manage their emotions, remain calm under pressure, and stay disciplined in following their strategies. By continuously honing these skills, traders increase their chances of consistent profitability, allowing them to steadily build wealth and achieve financial independence.

3. Case Studies of Traders Who Have Transformed Their Earnings

To illustrate the potential of unlimited income through trading, we'll look at some real-life examples of traders who have successfully scaled their earnings by mastering the markets:

Case Study 1: George Soros – The Billion-Dollar Bet

George Soros is perhaps one of the most famous traders in history. His most well-known trade was in 1992 when he "broke the Bank of England" by shorting the British pound. By leveraging his knowledge of economic trends and market timing, Soros made over $1 billion in a single trade. This trade highlighted how traders can capitalize on large market movements and make exponential gains when their analysis and timing align with the right opportunities.

Case Study 2: Paul Tudor Jones – Thriving in a Crisis

Paul Tudor Jones is renowned for his ability to profit during turbulent market conditions. In 1987, during the infamous Black Monday stock market crash, Jones predicted the collapse and took large short positions. His foresight and disciplined strategy helped him turn a massive profit while others were suffering significant losses. This case underscores the importance of strategy and risk management, especially during volatile times.

Case Study 3: Linda Raschke – Consistent Profits through Technical Mastery

Linda Raschke, a highly respected trader, is known for her technical analysis and disciplined approach to trading. She has consistently generated profits over her multi-decade career by sticking to her strategy and managing risk effectively. Her success story is a testament to how developing strong technical skills and emotional control can lead to steady, long-term profitability.

Case Study 4: Stanley Druckenmiller – Following Macro Trends

Stanley Druckenmiller, a protégé of George Soros, has made his fortune by identifying large macroeconomic trends and capitalizing on them through strategic trades. His ability to see the bigger picture and execute large trades has earned him billions over his career. Druckenmiller's success demonstrates how traders can profit by focusing on global economic trends and positioning themselves accordingly.

These case studies highlight that while trading offers immense earning potential, success is built on a foundation of skill development, strategy, and disciplined execution. It's not about luck or chance, but about leveraging knowledge and expertise to capitalize on opportunities in the market.

Conclusion

The potential to earn unlimited income is what makes trading one of the most compelling professions in the world. However, this potential is unlocked only through dedication to learning, skill development, and disciplined execution. As traders grow their expertise, they can scale their earnings to heights unimaginable in traditional careers. Through consistent learning, sound strategies, and emotional control, the dream of financial freedom through trading becomes a reality.

In the next chapter, we will explore how trading offers Freedom & Flexibility—allowing you to design a life on your own terms, working from anywhere in the world, and choosing your own schedule.

CHAPTER 3: FREEDOM & FLEXIBILITY – DESIGNING A LIFE ON YOUR TERMS

One of the greatest rewards of becoming a trader is the freedom it offers—freedom from office hours, geographical limitations, and rigid work schedules. In the modern world, where flexibility and work-life balance are increasingly valued, trading stands out as a profession that offers true autonomy. With just a smartphone and an internet connection, traders can operate from virtually anywhere, whether it's a bustling city, a beachside villa, or a quiet mountain retreat. This chapter explores the unique ways trading allows for location independence, the ability to balance life and work, and real-life examples of traders who have crafted their dream lifestyles.

Key Themes:

1. How Trading Enables Location Independence
Traditional careers often come with geographical restrictions. People are usually tied to office buildings, specific locations, or

rigid commuting schedules. However, trading completely shatters this limitation, as traders are only bound by their connection to the markets and access to technology. This profession allows for true location independence, meaning that you can work from anywhere in the world as long as you have a stable internet connection and a smartphone.

The key benefits of location independence in trading include:

Global Market Access: No matter where you are, you can access global financial markets, including forex, commodities, stocks, and cryptocurrencies. This means that whether you're in a small town or a metropolitan hub, you can trade in markets across time zones, providing constant opportunities.

The Freedom to Travel: Trading allows you to travel the world without being confined to a traditional office setup. Whether you're exploring a new city or lounging on a beach, you can check market trends, execute trades, and manage your portfolio on the go. This level of freedom is rare in most professions and can drastically enhance your quality of life.

Customizable Work Environment: Traders can design their ideal workspace—whether it's a home office, a coworking space, or even a café. Unlike conventional jobs that require office attendance, traders can adjust their surroundings to enhance productivity, creativity, and personal comfort.

This flexibility is especially appealing to those who prioritize work-life balance and want the freedom to choose where they live, how they work, and when they work. As a trader, you're in full control of your schedule and surroundings, empowering you to design a lifestyle that fits your personal preferences.

2. Balancing Life and Work Through Trading

One of the most attractive aspects of trading is the ability to balance life and work on your own terms. In contrast to a traditional 9-to-5 job, where work hours are predetermined and non-negotiable, trading allows you to structure your day based on your personal needs and goals. You're not limited by office hours, meetings, or deadlines set by others. Instead, you have the freedom to craft a schedule that suits your lifestyle.

Some key advantages of balancing life and work through trading include:

Flexible Work Hours: Financial markets operate across different time zones, allowing traders to select the hours that work best for them. Whether you prefer early mornings or late nights, trading gives you the flexibility to create a schedule that aligns with your personal rhythm.

Work When You're Most Productive: Instead of adhering to a company's schedule, you can work during the hours when you feel most focused and productive. This leads to increased efficiency and helps you avoid burnout.

More Time for Personal Pursuits: With the flexibility of trading, you have more time to dedicate to personal interests, hobbies, family, or travel. This balance allows for a more fulfilling lifestyle where work doesn't dominate your day, and you have the time to pursue the things that truly matter to you.

While trading does require focus and discipline, the beauty of the profession is that you can find a rhythm that blends work with life's other important aspects. Unlike rigid corporate structures, trading lets you align your work with your passions and priorities, creating a harmonious balance.

3. Real-Life Examples of Traders Living Their Dream Lifestyles
To showcase how trading can offer a dream lifestyle, let's look at some real-life examples of traders who have achieved freedom and flexibility through their work:

Case Study 1: Tim, the Digital Nomad Trader
Tim is a forex trader who turned his passion for traveling into a lifestyle of full-time global exploration. After mastering his trading strategy, he decided to pursue his dream of visiting countries across Asia, Europe, and South America. Tim's day starts early with a few hours of market analysis and trading, after which he's free to explore new cities, cultures, and landscapes. With just a smartphone and an internet connection, Tim is living his dream of seeing the world while sustaining his financial independence through trading.

Case Study 2: Sarah, the Stay-at-Home Parent
Sarah, a mother of two, chose trading as her profession to stay home with her children while still pursuing a career. Unlike traditional jobs that would have required her to put her children in daycare, trading has allowed her to design a schedule that works around her family's needs. She trades for a few hours during the day and uses market tools that let her manage positions without constantly being glued to her screen. Trading has given Sarah the ability to balance her role as a parent while maintaining financial independence.

Case Study 3: James, the Trader from Paradise
James built his trading career after leaving a stressful corporate job. He now lives on a tropical island, where he spends his mornings trading and his afternoons surfing. Trading has enabled him to live in a location that most people only dream of visiting on vacation. With low living expenses and high earnings from trading, James enjoys a lifestyle that is both fulfilling and financially sustainable. He works less than four hours a day, and the rest of the time is spent enjoying the beach, hiking, and indulging in his hobbies.

Case Study 4: Emily, the Part-Time Traveler
Emily works as a trader but considers herself more of a part-time

traveler. While she enjoys her home life, she also loves exploring new destinations for short periods. Trading gives her the freedom to take extended vacations without needing to take time off from work. Emily regularly spends weeks in different countries, working from her hotel room in the morning and exploring the local culture by the afternoon. Trading has given her a flexible income stream that fits seamlessly with her passion for travel.

These examples highlight how trading empowers individuals to live life on their own terms. Whether it's pursuing a nomadic lifestyle, balancing family commitments, or achieving financial independence while living in a dream location, the flexibility of trading makes it all possible. The key is that trading allows you to design a life that prioritizes what matters most to you, rather than being bound by a traditional office or job structure.

Conclusion
The freedom and flexibility that trading offers are among the most significant reasons it is considered the ultimate profession. With the ability to work from anywhere, control your schedule, and balance work with personal passions, trading offers the kind of lifestyle that many dream of, but few traditional careers can provide. By leveraging the autonomy that comes with trading, you can design a life on your own terms—whether that's traveling the world, spending more time with family, or simply living in a place that brings you joy. Trading is not just a profession; it's a gateway to personal freedom and limitless opportunities.

In the next chapter, we will dive into how trading gives you complete Independence, allowing you to take full control of your financial destiny without answering to anyone but yourself.

CHAPTER 4: INDEPENDENCE – THE POWER OF SELF-RELIANCE IN TRADING

One of the most empowering aspects of trading is the independence it provides. In traditional careers, your success is often tied to others—supervisors, teams, or corporate hierarchies. But in trading, you are your own boss. Every decision, every strategy, and every outcome rests solely in your hands. This chapter delves into the autonomy that trading fosters, the sense of empowerment that comes from making your own decisions, and how to manage the responsibilities that come with true independence.

Key Themes:

1. How Trading Fosters Self-Reliance
In trading, there's no need for a team meeting to get approval, no waiting for a superior to sign off on a project, and no workplace politics to navigate. Everything you do is up to you, and this is both liberating and challenging. Self-reliance in trading is a vital skill that, once mastered, can lead to immense personal and

financial freedom. It forces you to trust your own abilities and take full responsibility for your successes and failures.

Trading fosters self-reliance in several keyways:

Decision-Making Power: You're in charge of every trade you make —when to enter, when to exit, how much to risk, and what strategies to employ. This requires strong decision-making skills and the confidence to trust your judgment.

No Middle Management: In trading, you are not dependent on any corporate ladder or manager to determine your progress or success. You're not limited by someone else's evaluation of your worth or value. Your growth is in your hands, and you can move as fast as your skills allow.

Complete Control Over Learning and Growth: Traders must constantly refine their skills and strategies, but unlike a typical job where training is provided or mandated, traders are responsible for seeking out their own education. This could mean learning from books, courses, mentors, or personal experience. Self-reliance here means owning your learning journey and evolving continuously.

By fostering self-reliance, trading offers a path to not only financial independence but also personal growth. It challenges you to develop resilience, discipline, and emotional control—skills that can serve you well beyond the trading world.

2. The Empowerment of Making Your Own Decisions
In most professions, decision-making power is often diluted by company structures, team dynamics, or bureaucracy. In contrast, trading empowers you to make decisions swiftly and autonomously, giving you complete control over your financial future. This empowerment comes from being able to act on your own analysis, insights, and instincts without needing approval from others.

Key aspects of decision-making empowerment in trading include:

Real-Time Decision Making: Trading requires fast, independent decision-making. Whether you're executing a quick trade in the forex market or holding a position in stocks for weeks, the responsibility to make the right call at the right moment lies with you. This autonomy strengthens your ability to think clearly under pressure and trust your intuition.

Tailoring Strategies to Your Strengths: Every trader has their own strengths, weaknesses, and risk tolerance. Trading allows you to design strategies that are uniquely suited to you. For example, you might be someone who thrives in high-volatility markets, while another trader prefers a slower, long-term approach. This freedom to customize your trading style empowers you to operate in a way that aligns with your personal strengths and goals.

Learning From Your Decisions: Every trade, whether a success or failure, provides feedback. Because you are fully in control of your decisions, you can learn directly from the outcomes and adjust accordingly. This continuous feedback loop sharpens your ability to make better, more informed decisions over time.

The empowerment that comes from making your own decisions in trading is deeply rewarding. You gain confidence in your abilities and realize that your financial future is something you can shape on your own terms. This level of empowerment is rare in traditional professions, where decision-making is often shared or constrained by company policies.

3. Managing the Responsibilities of Independence

With great independence comes great responsibility. While trading offers unmatched freedom, it also demands discipline, self-management, and accountability. The success or failure of your trading career depends solely on your actions, which can be both exhilarating and daunting. Without a boss or team to guide you, you need to be diligent in managing your time, risk, and mindset.

Here's how you can effectively manage the responsibilities of independence in trading:

Discipline and Routine: Trading requires you to be disciplined, especially when there's no external structure to hold you accountable. Creating a routine is essential to staying focused and consistent. This could involve setting dedicated hours for market analysis, journaling your trades, and reviewing your strategies regularly. By establishing routines, you ensure that your trading business is treated with the same seriousness as any other profession.

Risk Management: One of the most critical responsibilities in trading is managing risk. Since you have complete control over your trades, you also bear full responsibility for protecting your capital. This involves setting strict risk limits, using stop-losses, and ensuring that you don't over-leverage your positions. Effective risk management is the cornerstone of long-term trading success, and it's something that traders must take seriously.

Handling Losses: In a traditional job, setbacks are often shared among teams or managed by supervisors. In trading, losses are personal and immediate. Every trader experiences losses, but how you handle them will determine your long-term success. The independence that comes with trading requires you to develop emotional resilience and not let losses impact your judgment. Learning to accept and learn from losses is a key part of managing your independence as a trader.

Self-Motivation: With no boss breathing down your neck, it's easy to become complacent or distracted. Traders must be self-motivated to continually improve their skills, adapt to market changes, and stay disciplined even during periods of stagnation. Motivation must come from within, driven by your goals and vision for the future.

The responsibility that comes with trading independence is immense, but it is also highly rewarding. Managing this responsibility effectively not only enhances your trading results but also builds character, resilience, and leadership qualities that can be applied in all areas of life.

Conclusion

The independence that trading provides is unparalleled in comparison to traditional professions. It fosters self-reliance, grants you the empowerment to make your own decisions, and challenges you to manage the responsibilities that come with autonomy. In trading, you are in complete control of your financial destiny, which is both the greatest opportunity and the greatest challenge.

By embracing this independence and refining your skills, you can build a career that is not just financially rewarding but also deeply fulfilling. Trading gives you the freedom to design your own path, without relying on anyone else. As we explore in the next chapter, this independence also leads to another significant benefit—low barriers to entry, which make trading accessible to anyone willing to learn and put in the work.

CHAPTER 5: LOW BARRIERS TO ENTRY – OPPORTUNITY FOR EVERYONE

One of the most exciting aspects of trading is its accessibility. Unlike many professions that require years of formal education, expensive degrees, or large financial investments, trading offers a straightforward path to entry with minimal upfront costs. In today's digital world, practically anyone with an internet connection and the willingness to learn can begin their journey in the financial markets. This chapter highlights the low barriers to entry in trading and emphasizes how almost anyone, regardless of background or experience, can enter the world of trading with the right mindset and approach.

Key Themes:

1. What You Need to Get Started
Starting a career in trading is simpler than many other professions. You don't need to attend a prestigious university, accumulate certifications, or invest a fortune in equipment and office space. The basic tools for getting started as a trader are

readily available and accessible to most people.

Here's what you need to begin trading:

A Computer or Mobile Device: Any modern computer, laptop, or even a smartphone will suffice for most trading activities. You don't need to invest in a high-end system; if your device has an internet connection and can run trading platforms smoothly, you're good to go.

Internet Connection: A stable internet connection is crucial, especially if you're engaging in short-term or day trading where timely execution of trades is important. Fortunately, most people already have access to reliable internet, and this makes trading accessible from virtually anywhere in the world.

Trading Platform: To place trades, you'll need access to a trading platform or broker. There are countless online brokers available today, many of which offer free accounts or minimal fees for new traders. Platforms like MetaTrader or brokerage apps like JustMarkets provide user-friendly interfaces that allow you to trade various asset classes, such as forex, stocks, commodities, and cryptocurrencies.

Starting Capital: One of the most common misconceptions about trading is that you need a large sum of money to start. This isn't the case. Thanks to the accessibility of online brokers, you can open an account with as little as $100 and begin trading. Many brokers also offer leverage, which allows you to control a larger position with a small amount of capital, although this should be used with caution.

Education and Learning Resources: The key to succeeding in trading isn't having a lot of money but having the knowledge and skills to navigate the markets. Thankfully, there's a wealth of free or affordable educational resources available online, from

YouTube videos and trading blogs to online courses and webinars. With dedication and consistent study, anyone can learn the basics of trading and work their way toward more advanced strategies.

These low requirements mean that virtually anyone can start trading, regardless of financial background or formal education. The accessibility of these tools makes trading one of the few professions where the barriers to entry are not limited by geography, social status, or prior experience.

2. Cost-Effective Ways to Enter the Trading World

Getting into trading doesn't have to break the bank. In fact, there are several cost-effective ways to start learning and trading without putting significant financial resources at risk. In this section, we'll explore how to minimize costs while maximizing your learning potential.

Some affordable entry points into trading include:

Demo Accounts: One of the best ways to start learning how to trade without risking any real money is by using a demo account. Most trading platforms offer demo accounts that simulate real market conditions. This allows you to practice trading strategies, understand market movements, and build confidence without the fear of losing real capital. Using a demo account is an excellent way to get a feel for the markets while preserving your funds for when you're ready to trade live.

Micro Accounts: Once you've practiced on a demo account and feel ready to trade with real money, consider starting with a micro or mini account. These types of accounts allow you to trade smaller position sizes, meaning your potential losses are limited, while still gaining experience with real market conditions. Micro accounts often require low minimum deposits and provide an affordable way to start live trading.

Educational Resources: You don't need to spend thousands of dollars on expensive courses or seminars to learn how to trade. There are plenty of free or low-cost educational resources available online. Websites like BabyPips offer comprehensive beginner's guides to forex trading, while platforms like Udemy or Coursera provide affordable courses on technical analysis, trading psychology, and risk management. Many successful traders have built their skills using self-directed, cost-effective learning strategies.

Leverage Free Content: The internet is filled with free content from experienced traders sharing their insights. Whether it's blogs, YouTube tutorials, or podcasts, you can access a wealth of knowledge without spending a dime. Following successful traders on social media platforms or joining trading communities can also provide valuable tips and advice, often at no cost.
By leveraging these affordable tools and resources, you can gain experience and knowledge without needing a large financial commitment upfront. This approach allows you to enter the trading world at a pace that suits your budget while minimizing risk.

3. How to Build Skills Without Significant Financial Risk
One of the fears many aspiring traders have is the risk of losing money before they've had a chance to build their skills. While trading does involve risk, there are several ways to mitigate this and learn the craft without jeopardizing your financial security.

Key strategies to build skills without significant financial risk include:

Start Small: When you're first starting out, it's important to trade with money you can afford to lose. Start with a small amount of capital, so that even if things don't go as planned, your financial stability won't be impacted. This also allows you to focus on the learning process rather than the fear of losing large sums.

Practice with a Demo Account: As mentioned earlier, demo accounts are invaluable for building skills without any financial risk. Spend time experimenting with different strategies, learning from mistakes, and fine-tuning your approach before you start trading with real money.

Risk Management Techniques: Proper risk management is critical to long-term success in trading. Use stop-loss orders to limit potential losses and ensure you never risk more than a small percentage of your capital on any single trade. For new traders, this is typically around 1% to 2% of their total capital. By limiting your downside, you can weather losses while still learning and improving.

Use Leverage Responsibly: While leverage can amplify your gains, it can also increase your losses if not used carefully. When starting out, it's advisable to use minimal or no leverage to reduce your risk. As you build your skills and confidence, you can gradually incorporate leverage into your trading strategy, but always with caution and proper risk management.

Track and Analyse Your Trades: Keeping a trading journal is one of the most effective ways to improve your skills without financial risk. By tracking every trade you make, noting your strategy, emotions, and outcomes, you can identify patterns, learn from mistakes, and refine your approach. This form of self-reflection is an essential part of growing as a trader and can prevent you from repeating costly errors.

By starting small, practicing risk management, and continuously improving through reflection and analysis, you can build your trading skills while minimizing financial exposure. Trading is a journey that requires patience and discipline, but by managing risk effectively, you can grow your knowledge and experience without facing catastrophic losses.

Conclusion

The low barriers to entry in trading make it a unique and accessible opportunity for anyone willing to learn. With minimal upfront costs, affordable learning resources, and strategies to manage risk, trading offers a path for those who want to take control of their financial future without needing significant financial backing or years of formal education.

The real challenge is not the financial entry point but the dedication to learning and the discipline to manage risk effectively. By leveraging demo accounts, starting with small investments, and continuously honing your skills, you can enter the world of trading with confidence.

In the next chapter, we'll explore how Constant Learning & Growth are key components of trading success, and why the learning process in trading never truly ends, keeping you engaged and evolving throughout your journey.

CHAPTER 6: CONSTANT LEARNING – EMBRACING THE LIFELONG JOURNEY OF GROWTH

Trading is not a static profession; it is a dynamic and ever-evolving landscape that demands a commitment to continuous learning. Market conditions change, technology advances, and global events influence financial markets in real-time. To succeed in this environment, traders must embrace the idea that learning is a lifelong journey. This chapter explores how the nature of trading necessitates ongoing education and personal growth, and how successful traders adapt and evolve with the markets.

Key Themes:

1. How Market Conditions Drive Continuous Learning
The financial markets are influenced by a myriad of factors, including economic indicators, geopolitical events, interest rates,

and technological advancements. Each of these elements can significantly impact market behaviour, and to be successful, traders must stay informed and adjust their strategies accordingly.

Key aspects of how market conditions drive continuous learning include:

Adapting to Volatility: Market volatility can arise from various factors, such as unexpected news events, changes in economic policy, or shifts in investor sentiment. Successful traders recognize that they must constantly analyse and adapt to these conditions. This requires them to stay updated on market news and trends, adjusting their strategies in real time to capitalize on new opportunities or mitigate risks.

Understanding Economic Indicators: Traders need to have a firm grasp of key economic indicators—such as GDP, unemployment rates, inflation, and central bank policies—that influence market movements. As these indicators evolve and impact the markets, traders must learn to interpret their significance and make informed trading decisions based on this information.

Responding to Technological Changes: Advances in technology can drastically change how trading is conducted. From high-frequency trading algorithms to AI-driven market analysis tools, technology is reshaping the trading landscape. Successful traders must keep pace with these advancements, learning to use new tools and platforms that can enhance their trading effectiveness.

Recognizing Behavioural Patterns: Market psychology plays a crucial role in trading. Traders must understand how emotions —both their own and those of the broader market—impact price movements. This requires ongoing analysis of market sentiment, learning to recognize patterns of behaviour, and adjusting strategies to account for the psychology of traders in the market.

In an ever-changing environment, traders who commit to continual learning will not only adapt to market shifts but also develop a deeper understanding of the intricate dynamics at play.

2. Staying Ahead of the Curve with Education

To thrive in the competitive world of trading, education is paramount. The best traders recognize that they cannot afford to become complacent with their knowledge; they must proactively seek out new information and insights to stay ahead of their peers. This chapter emphasizes the importance of ongoing education and staying current with market trends.

Ways to stay ahead of the curve include:

Participating in Online Courses and Webinars: There are numerous online platforms offering courses tailored for traders of all skill levels. These courses often cover a wide range of topics —from technical analysis and trading psychology to advanced strategies for specific markets. Webinars hosted by experienced traders can also provide valuable insights and the latest trends in trading techniques.

Reading Books and Articles: The literature available on trading is vast. Reading books written by successful traders, market analysts, and economists can provide invaluable knowledge and unique perspectives. Articles from reputable financial news sources can also keep you informed about recent market developments and strategies.

Joining Trading Communities: Engaging with fellow traders in online forums or local trading groups can provide a wealth of shared knowledge and experiences. Discussing strategies, sharing successes and failures, and asking questions can greatly enhance your learning process. Many successful traders are willing to share their insights and mentor others, creating an enriching environment for learning.

Networking with Other Traders: Networking can open opportunities to learn from experienced traders and industry professionals. Attending trading conferences, workshops, or meetups allows you to gain insights from the best in the business while also sharing your experiences. Building relationships with other traders can lead to collaborations, mentorship, and knowledge exchange that can significantly enhance your trading skill set.

By prioritizing education and actively seeking knowledge, traders position themselves to adapt to the ever-changing landscape of financial markets. Continuous education is not just a way to keep pace with the competition; it's an essential component of becoming a successful trader.

3. Tools and Resources for Traders to Keep Learning

The trading community is rich with resources designed to aid ongoing learning and development. These tools and resources range from analytical software to educational platforms, and they can play a critical role in enhancing a trader's skill set and understanding of the markets.

Essential tools and resources for continuous learning include:

Trading Platforms with Educational Features: Many modern trading platforms offer integrated educational resources, such as tutorials, market analysis, and real-time data feeds. Utilizing these features can help traders stay informed about market conditions and refine their strategies.

Market Analysis Tools: Access to tools like charting software, technical indicators, and economic calendars can aid traders in making informed decisions. Understanding how to utilize these tools effectively requires ongoing practice and study, but they can provide significant advantages when analysing market trends and potential trading opportunities.

Simulation Software: Besides demo accounts, simulation software allows traders to practice trading strategies in real-time market conditions without risking actual capital. These platforms often provide scenarios that mimic various market situations, allowing traders to develop their skills and build confidence before trading with real money.

Podcasts and Video Channels: Many successful traders and financial analysts host podcasts or YouTube channels dedicated to trading education. These platforms often cover a wide array of topics, including strategies, psychological aspects of trading, and interviews with industry professionals. Listening to or watching these resources can provide fresh insights and keep traders motivated.

Online Trading Journals: Using digital trading journals can help traders track their progress, analyse their decisions, and document lessons learned. This practice not only encourages self-reflection but also helps traders identify patterns in their behaviour and decision-making processes, leading to continuous improvement.

By leveraging these tools and resources, traders can create a robust learning environment that fosters growth and adaptability. The commitment to continuous learning ultimately leads to a deeper understanding of market mechanics and improved trading performance.

Conclusion

In the fast-paced world of trading, the commitment to constant learning is essential for success. Market conditions continuously evolve, requiring traders to adapt and grow in their knowledge and skills. By recognizing the importance of ongoing education, leveraging available resources, and staying informed about market trends, traders can position themselves for long-term success.

The journey of a trader is a lifelong process of growth, filled with challenges and opportunities for learning. In the next chapter, we will explore Personal Development & Growth, emphasizing how trading not only shapes your financial future but also contributes to your overall character and resilience.

CHAPTER 7: PERSONAL DEVELOPMENT – BUILDING RESILIENCE, DISCIPLINE, AND EMOTIONAL CONTROL

Trading is often perceived as a technical pursuit, focused primarily on numbers, charts, and market movements. However, beneath the surface lies a profound journey of personal development that shapes not only your trading abilities but also your character and approach to life. As traders navigate the highs and lows of the market, they inevitably cultivate essential personal attributes such as emotional control, discipline, and resilience. This chapter delves into how these qualities are crucial for achieving success in trading and how they contribute to overall personal growth.

Key Themes:

1. Emotional Management During Wins and Losses

In trading, emotions can significantly impact decision-making and performance. The ability to manage emotions—whether during winning streaks or inevitable losses—is vital for long-term success.

Key aspects of emotional management include:

Recognizing Emotional Triggers: Successful traders are adept at identifying their emotional triggers. Whether it's the exhilaration of a big win or the frustration of a loss, recognizing these feelings is the first step in managing them. By being aware of how emotions influence decisions, traders can develop strategies to remain level-headed in both profitable and challenging situations.

Staying Objective: Emotional responses can cloud judgment. Traders who learn to separate their feelings from their trading decisions can make more rational choices. Techniques such as mindfulness and self-reflection can help maintain objectivity, allowing traders to assess situations based on facts rather than emotions.

Implementing a Trading Plan: A well-defined trading plan acts as a roadmap, providing guidelines on when to enter or exit trades. Sticking to this plan, regardless of emotional states, helps mitigate impulsive decisions driven by fear or greed. This discipline ensures that traders remain focused on their long-term goals rather than short-term emotional reactions.

Accepting Losses: Losses are an inevitable part of trading. Developing emotional resilience means learning to accept losses as part of the journey rather than viewing them as failures. This acceptance allows traders to move forward, analyze what went wrong, and refine their strategies without dwelling on negative experiences.

Emotional management is not only essential for trading but also applies to other aspects of life. Learning to regulate emotions during stressful situations leads to greater resilience and adaptability in various contexts.

2. Building Resilience and Mental Toughness

Resilience is the ability to bounce back from setbacks, and mental toughness is the strength of mind to persist in the face of challenges. Both qualities are crucial for traders who face unpredictable market fluctuations and the psychological pressures that come with them.

Key elements of building resilience and mental toughness include:

Learning from Failure: Instead of viewing setbacks as defeats, successful traders see them as opportunities for growth. Analysing past mistakes and understanding what went wrong enables traders to make necessary adjustments and avoid repeating those errors in the future. This mindset fosters resilience and prepares them for future challenges.

Developing a Growth Mindset: Embracing a growth mindset—the belief that abilities and intelligence can be developed through hard work and dedication—empowers traders to view challenges as opportunities to learn rather than obstacles. This perspective encourages continuous improvement and a willingness to adapt to changing market conditions.

Practicing Patience and Persistence: Trading requires patience, as profits may take time to materialize. Resilient traders learn to wait for the right opportunities and are persistent in their pursuit of success. They understand that consistency, rather than immediate results, is the key to achieving long-term goals.

Stress Management Techniques: Engaging in practices such as meditation, exercise, or other forms of self-care can help traders manage stress levels. A healthy body and mind are essential for maintaining focus and clarity in decision-making, especially during challenging market conditions.

By cultivating resilience and mental toughness, traders can navigate the ups and downs of trading with a greater sense of confidence and determination. These attributes not only enhance trading performance but also contribute to overall personal well-being and effectiveness in other areas of life.

3. How Trading Discipline Translates into Personal Growth

Discipline is at the core of successful trading. It involves adhering to a well-defined trading plan, managing risk effectively, and maintaining consistent behaviour in decision-making. This discipline fosters personal growth in several ways.

Key insights into how trading discipline translates into personal growth include:

Setting Goals and Accountability: Traders often set specific, measurable goals to guide their trading journey. This process of goal-setting fosters accountability and encourages traders to track their progress. As they achieve these goals, they build confidence and a sense of accomplishment that spills over into other areas of life.

Time Management: Successful trading requires effective time management skills. Traders must allocate time for research, strategy development, and market analysis. Learning to manage time efficiently in trading can translate into improved time management in personal and professional life, leading to enhanced productivity.

Building Confidence through Routine: Establishing a disciplined routine—such as regular analysis of trades, continuous education, and maintaining a trading journal—helps build confidence. Consistent routines create a sense of stability, enabling traders to make more informed decisions and approach challenges with a positive mindset.

Learning Delayed Gratification: Trading often requires waiting for the right opportunities and accepting that immediate rewards may not always be attainable. This practice of delayed gratification can lead to greater patience and long-term thinking in other aspects of life, whether in personal relationships, career pursuits, or financial planning.

Through trading discipline, individuals can cultivate habits that promote personal growth and development, equipping them with the tools to tackle challenges in various domains of life.

Conclusion

The journey of trading is intricately tied to personal development, shaping individuals into more resilient, disciplined, and emotionally intelligent beings. By mastering emotional management, building resilience, and embracing discipline, traders not only enhance their trading performance but also develop critical life skills that contribute to their overall growth and well-being.

In the next chapter, we will explore the Instant Feedback for Improvement, emphasizing how the unique feedback loop in trading fosters rapid learning and improvement, allowing traders to refine their skills and strategies continuously.

CHAPTER 8: INSTANT FEEDBACK – RAPID IMPROVEMENT AND REFINING YOUR STRATEGY

In the fast-paced world of trading, one of the most powerful advantages is the ability to receive immediate feedback on your actions. Unlike many professions where the outcomes of decisions may take time to materialize, traders experience a quick and tangible response to their strategies. This instant feedback loop allows traders to make real-time adjustments, learn from their successes and failures, and continuously refine their trading strategies. In this chapter, we will explore how traders can harness the power of instant feedback to enhance their performance and develop more effective trading approaches.

Key Themes:

1. The Benefits of a Quick Feedback Loop
The immediacy of feedback in trading provides several unique

benefits that can significantly enhance a trader's ability to learn and adapt:

Accelerated Learning Curve: With instant feedback, traders can quickly determine what works and what doesn't. This rapid learning process enables them to understand market dynamics and refine their strategies more efficiently than in many other professions. By analysing the results of each trade immediately, traders can identify patterns and gain insights into their decision-making processes, leading to accelerated skill development.

Informed Decision-Making: The ability to see the direct consequences of a trading decision fosters a culture of informed decision-making. Traders can assess the effectiveness of their strategies and adjust on the fly. This immediacy helps to reinforce positive behaviours and discourage unproductive ones, ultimately leading to better trading practices.

Emotional Regulation: Instant feedback allows traders to learn how to manage their emotions effectively. By observing how their emotional states impact their trading decisions and outcomes, traders can develop better emotional control. This understanding can help mitigate impulsive decisions based on fear or greed, leading to more disciplined trading behaviour.

Building Confidence: Receiving immediate feedback on trades—whether successful or not—helps build confidence. When traders see positive results from their strategies, it reinforces their belief in their abilities. Conversely, understanding why a trade didn't go as planned provides an opportunity to learn without feeling defeated, contributing to a more resilient mindset.

2. Refining Strategies with Real-Time Results
The capacity to analyse trades in real time is invaluable for refining strategies. This section explores how traders can leverage instant feedback to enhance their trading approaches:

Evaluating Trade Performance: After each trade, successful traders take time to evaluate their performance. They analyse the entry and exit points, the timing of their decisions, and the overall effectiveness of their strategy. By maintaining a trading journal, traders can document the reasoning behind each trade and the resulting feedback, facilitating deeper insights into their trading patterns.

Adapting to Market Conditions: Financial markets are inherently dynamic and can change rapidly. The ability to receive immediate feedback allows traders to adapt their strategies to current market conditions. For example, if a particular trading strategy is not yielding the expected results, traders can quickly pivot to alternative approaches that may be more effective under the current circumstances.

Back testing Strategies: Instant feedback can also enhance the process of back testing trading strategies. By simulating trades based on historical data, traders can observe how their strategies would have performed under various market conditions. This process provides valuable insights that can lead to the refinement of strategies before applying them in real-time trading.

Continuous Improvement: Traders who actively seek feedback from their trades cultivate a mindset of continuous improvement. By reviewing both winning and losing trades, they can identify strengths and weaknesses in their strategies. This commitment to improvement fosters a growth mindset, encouraging traders to remain open to change and innovation in their approach.

3. How to Apply Lessons from Feedback

Receiving instant feedback is only part of the equation; the real challenge lies in effectively applying the lessons learned. This section highlights how traders can incorporate feedback into their ongoing development:

Establishing a Feedback Loop: To make the most of instant feedback, traders should create a structured feedback loop. This can involve setting aside time after each trading session to review trades, analyze outcomes, and identify areas for improvement. By establishing a routine for feedback analysis, traders ensure that they consistently integrate lessons learned into their strategies.

Identifying Key Performance Indicators (KPIs): Traders should define specific KPIs to measure their performance objectively. These might include metrics such as win rate, average profit/loss per trade, or risk-reward ratios. By tracking these indicators over time, traders can gain insights into their performance and identify trends that inform future trading decisions.

Adopting a Reflective Mindset: A reflective mindset is crucial for applying feedback effectively. Traders should be willing to critically assess their decisions and be honest about their strengths and weaknesses. This self-reflection fosters personal growth and helps traders learn from their experiences, ultimately leading to more informed and confident trading decisions.

Creating Actionable Plans: After analysing feedback, traders should develop actionable plans to implement improvements. This might involve adjusting their trading strategies, refining their risk management techniques, or enhancing their emotional control practices. By creating specific, measurable action plans, traders can take tangible steps toward continuous improvement.

Conclusion

The ability to receive instant feedback is one of trading's most significant advantages, allowing traders to learn rapidly, refine their strategies, and enhance their performance. By leveraging this feedback loop effectively, traders can accelerate their growth and adapt to the ever-changing market landscape.

As we move forward, the next chapter will focus on Access to Global Markets & Liquidity, highlighting the vast opportunities available to traders and how they can harness the liquidity of global markets to maximize their potential for success.

CHAPTER 9: GLOBAL MARKETS & LIQUIDITY – TAPPING INTO WORLDWIDE OPPORTUNITIES

In the realm of trading, the world truly becomes your marketplace. The globalization of finance has opened countless avenues for traders to explore, offering a diverse range of assets, from traditional commodities to innovative cryptocurrencies. This chapter delves into how global markets provide traders with endless opportunities and emphasizes the importance of liquidity in capitalizing on these prospects. By understanding how to navigate these markets, traders can position themselves for success and leverage the unique advantages that come with operating on a global scale.

Key Themes:

1. Overview of Global Markets and Their Accessibility
The landscape of global markets is vast and varied, encompassing

a multitude of asset classes and trading platforms that cater to traders of all experience levels.

Diverse Asset Classes: Global markets offer a wide array of asset classes, including stocks, bonds, commodities, currencies, and cryptocurrencies. Each asset class presents unique characteristics and trading opportunities, allowing traders to diversify their portfolios and manage risk effectively. For instance, forex trading enables participants to trade currency pairs, while commodity trading allows for investment in physical goods like gold and oil.

24/5 Trading Accessibility: Unlike traditional markets that operate within specific hours, many global markets are open around the clock, allowing traders to engage in trading activities at any time. This 24/5 structure means that traders can react to news, market developments, or economic indicators as they happen, regardless of their geographical location. This flexibility is particularly advantageous for those who wish to trade part-time or from different time zones.

Technological Advancements: The rise of online trading platforms and mobile applications has further democratized access to global markets. Traders can now execute trades, analyse market data, and monitor their portfolios from virtually anywhere in the world. This increased accessibility empowers individuals to participate in trading without the need for a physical presence on trading floors or through traditional brokerage firms.

Regulatory Considerations: While global markets offer tremendous opportunities, traders must also be aware of the regulatory landscape. Different countries have varying regulations governing trading activities, and understanding these rules is essential for compliant trading. Familiarizing oneself with these regulations can help traders avoid potential pitfalls and ensure a smooth trading experience.

2. How Liquidity Works in Trading

Liquidity is a crucial factor in trading that impacts how easily assets can be bought or sold without significantly affecting their price.

Definition of Liquidity: In trading, liquidity refers to the ease with which an asset can be converted into cash without causing a drastic change in its price. Highly liquid markets, such as forex, enable traders to execute large orders swiftly, while illiquid markets may require more time and potentially lead to unfavourable price changes.

Market Makers and Participants: Liquidity is often provided by market makers, financial institutions that facilitate trading by providing buy and sell quotes. Their presence ensures that there is always a buyer or seller available, reducing the bid-ask spread and enhancing trading efficiency. In highly liquid markets, there are numerous participants, including institutional investors, retail traders, and algorithms, all contributing to market depth.

Impact of Liquidity on Trading Strategies: Traders should consider liquidity when developing their strategies. High liquidity allows for tighter spreads and faster execution of trades, making it ideal for day traders and scalpers who rely on quick price movements. Conversely, traders focusing on longer-term strategies may be less affected by liquidity, though they should still be mindful of market conditions that could impact their positions.

Liquidity Events: Certain market events can significantly influence liquidity, such as economic data releases, geopolitical developments, or major market news. Understanding how these events impact liquidity can help traders anticipate price movements and adjust their strategies accordingly. For instance, during high-impact news releases, liquidity may temporarily decrease, leading to wider spreads and increased volatility.

3. Leveraging Opportunities Across Time Zones and Regions

Global markets operate across various time zones, creating unique opportunities for traders to engage in trading activities at any hour.

Trading Around the Clock: The ability to trade in different time zones allows traders to capitalize on opportunities as they arise in various markets. For example, when the Asian markets close, the European markets open, followed by the U.S. markets. This continuous cycle enables traders to react to global news and developments, regardless of their local market hours.

Exploiting Regional Events: Different regions experience distinct economic conditions, cultural influences, and political climates that can create unique trading opportunities. Traders who stay informed about regional developments can make strategic decisions based on how these factors may affect asset prices. For instance, a political election in a major economy can influence currency values, creating potential trading opportunities for forex traders.

Adapting to Market Sentiment: Market sentiment can vary significantly across regions and time zones. By monitoring sentiment indicators and trading volume, traders can gauge potential market movements and adjust their strategies accordingly. Understanding how different regions respond to global events can provide valuable insights for making informed trading decisions.

Collaborative Trading Communities: With the global nature of trading, traders can connect with communities across the world. Online forums, social media, and trading groups allow individuals to share insights, strategies, and market analyses. Engaging with a diverse range of traders fosters collaboration and can enhance one's understanding of different markets and trading styles.

Conclusion

The vastness of global markets and their inherent liquidity create a wealth of opportunities for traders to explore. By understanding how to navigate these markets effectively, traders can position themselves to capitalize on diverse assets and react quickly to global developments. The ability to trade around the clock and leverage insights from various regions enhances the potential for success, making global markets a vital aspect of the trading profession.

In the upcoming chapter, we will discuss Impactful Wealth Creation, focusing on how trading not only leads to personal financial success but also allows individuals to create meaningful wealth that can positively impact their communities and future generations.

CHAPTER 10: IMPACTFUL WEALTH CREATION – TRADING BEYOND FINANCIAL GAINS

Trading is often viewed primarily as a vehicle for personal financial growth, yet its potential extends far beyond individual profit. Successful traders can leverage their financial gains to create a ripple effect that positively impacts their families, communities, and even the world. This chapter explores how trading can serve as a powerful catalyst for wealth creation that enriches not only the trader's life but also the lives of others, fostering a culture of giving back, empowerment, and social responsibility.

Key Themes:

1. The Ripple Effect of Wealth Creation
The impact of wealth creation through trading is not confined to the individual trader; it extends outward, influencing a broader

network of people and communities.

Financial Security for Families: Successful traders often achieve financial independence that allows them to provide for their families in ways that may not have been possible before. This financial security can lead to better education opportunities, improved living conditions, and a more comfortable lifestyle for loved ones. When traders share their financial knowledge and resources with their families, they contribute to a legacy of wealth that can span generations.

Economic Empowerment of Communities: As traders build their wealth, they can invest in their communities. This can involve supporting local businesses, providing jobs, or funding community projects that improve quality of life. Such investments can stimulate local economies, creating a positive cycle of growth and opportunity for others.

Inspiring Others: The success stories of traders can serve as powerful inspiration for those around them. By demonstrating what is possible through hard work, dedication, and strategic trading, successful individuals can motivate others to pursue their own financial goals. This ripple effect can create a culture of aspiration and achievement, encouraging others to invest in their financial education and take control of their economic futures.

2. Using Trading Profits for Charitable Causes

Many traders find fulfilment in using their trading profits to support charitable causes, recognizing that financial success brings with it the responsibility to give back.

Philanthropic Endeavours: Traders who achieve significant financial success often channel a portion of their profits into charitable initiatives. This can range from supporting local charities to establishing their own foundations focused on specific issues, such as education, health care, or environmental sustainability. By aligning their financial success with meaningful causes, traders can make a tangible difference in the lives of those in need.

Funding Educational Programs: One impactful way traders can give back is by funding educational programs that empower others with financial literacy and trading skills. This not only equips individuals with the tools to succeed but also fosters a more informed community that can make smarter financial decisions. Supporting initiatives that teach trading and investment strategies can create a legacy of knowledge and empowerment for future generations.

Social Entrepreneurship: Successful traders may also choose to invest in social enterprises—businesses that prioritize social impact alongside profit. By supporting ventures that tackle social challenges while generating revenue, traders can create sustainable change and contribute to a better world. This form of giving back blends entrepreneurship with philanthropy, resulting in a dual impact.

3. Empowering Others Through Trading Knowledge

Beyond financial contributions, traders can make a significant impact by sharing their knowledge and expertise with others.

Mentorship and Coaching: Experienced traders have a wealth of knowledge to share. By mentoring aspiring traders, they can help others navigate the complexities of the market, develop trading strategies, and avoid common pitfalls. This form of guidance not only fosters individual success but also strengthens the trading community.

Creating Educational Content: Traders can create online courses, webinars, or write books that provide insights into trading strategies, risk management, and market analysis. By disseminating this knowledge, they can empower others to take charge of their financial futures and make informed trading decisions. Educational content serves as a valuable resource for both beginners and experienced traders looking to refine their skills.

Building a Community: By fostering a supportive trading community, successful traders can create an environment where knowledge sharing is encouraged. Online forums, social media groups, and local trading meetups can facilitate discussions, promote collaboration, and provide opportunities for traders to learn from one another. Building a community cantered around growth and education can lead to collective success and support.

Conclusion
The journey of a trader extends far beyond personal financial gains. By recognizing the ripple effect of wealth creation, engaging in charitable initiatives, and empowering others through knowledge, traders can leverage their success to make a lasting impact on their families, communities, and the world at large. As we conclude this exploration of impactful wealth creation, it is essential to understand that trading is not just about numbers on a screen; it is about the lives we touch and the legacies we leave behind.
In the final chapter, we will discuss the importance of Legacy, focusing on how traders can pass down their knowledge and experiences to future generations, ensuring that the benefits of trading continue to flourish in the years to come.

CHAPTER 11: LEGACY – PASSING ON KNOWLEDGE AND BUILDING A FUTURE

The journey of a trader is often viewed as a personal quest for financial success, but the impact of that journey can extend far beyond the individual. A trader's legacy is not merely defined by their own accomplishments but also by their ability to inspire and empower future generations. In this chapter, we will explore the importance of leaving a legacy through mentorship, the significance of building a future for upcoming traders, and the methods by which traders can pass down valuable principles and strategies that foster continued success.

Key Themes:

1. Mentorship and Teaching as a Trader
Mentorship is a vital aspect of creating a legacy, as it allows seasoned traders to impart their knowledge and experience to aspiring traders.

The Role of a Mentor: Mentorship involves guiding newcomers through the complexities of trading, helping them navigate the challenges, and celebrating their successes. A mentor's support can make a significant difference in a beginner's confidence and understanding of the market. By sharing personal experiences, mentors can illustrate both the rewards and risks of trading, preparing their mentees for real-world scenarios.

Creating Educational Opportunities: Successful traders can establish formal or informal teaching programs, offering workshops, webinars, or online courses to educate aspiring traders. These programs can cover everything from basic trading principles to advanced strategies and risk management techniques. By providing structured learning opportunities, mentors can enhance the knowledge, and skill sets of future traders.

Fostering a Culture of Learning: Mentorship is about creating a culture that values continuous learning and growth. By encouraging their mentees to seek knowledge, ask questions, and share experiences, mentors help cultivate a community of informed traders who are committed to improving their skills and supporting one another.

2. Building a Legacy for Future Traders
A trader's legacy can manifest in various forms, providing long-term benefits to the trading community and society at large.

Establishing Organizations or Funds: Successful traders may choose to create organizations, scholarships, or trading funds aimed at supporting underprivileged individuals interested in trading. These initiatives can provide financial assistance, education, and mentorship to those who might not otherwise have access to such resources. By investing in future traders, they help ensure that talented individuals can succeed, regardless of their background.

Community Engagement: Building a legacy involves actively engaging with the trading community. Traders can organize local meetups, online forums, or events where experienced and novice traders can come together to share knowledge and experiences. This engagement not only strengthens the community but also establishes a supportive environment that encourages growth and collaboration.

Documenting Experiences and Insights: Sharing personal stories, lessons learned, and trading strategies through blogs, books, or video content can help create a legacy. Documenting experiences allows future traders to benefit from the wisdom of those who came before them, giving them a roadmap to navigate their own trading journeys.

3. Passing Down Principles and Strategies
The principles and strategies that guide a trader's success are invaluable resources that should be passed down to future generations.

Developing Core Trading Principles: Successful traders often develop a set of core principles that guide their decision-making process. These principles can include risk management, emotional control, and the importance of continuous learning. By articulating these values, traders can instil a strong foundation in their mentees, equipping them to navigate the ups and downs of trading.

Sharing Proven Strategies: Experienced traders have tested various strategies throughout their careers. Sharing these successful approaches, along with the rationale behind them, provides valuable insights for future traders. This knowledge transfer enables newcomers to learn from the successes and mistakes of others, accelerating their learning curve.

Encouraging Adaptability: While it's essential to share established principles and strategies, it's equally important to emphasize the need for adaptability. Markets are constantly evolving, and traders must be prepared to adjust their approaches in response to new information and changing conditions. Encouraging future traders to be open to change fosters a mindset that values innovation and resilience.

Conclusion
Leaving a legacy as a trader is about more than personal achievements; it's about shaping the future of the trading community by empowering others with knowledge, support, and opportunities. Through mentorship, the establishment of initiatives that benefit future traders, and the sharing of principles and strategies, successful traders can create a lasting impact that extends well beyond their own trading careers.
In this chapter, we have explored how the journey of a trader can evolve into a mission to educate and empower future generations. The final reflections will emphasize the importance of continuing the journey, as every trader has the potential to influence and inspire others, ensuring that the legacy of trading knowledge and success endures for years to come.

CHAPTER 12: CONCLUSION – YOUR JOURNEY STARTS NOW

Trading can unlock a life of freedom, wealth, and personal growth. The journey is challenging but deeply rewarding. In this final chapter, I offer encouragement and insights to help you take the next step on your trading path, equipped with the knowledge and mindset for success.

CHAPTER 12:
CONCLUSION -
YOUR JOURNEY
STARTS NOW

EPILOGUE

As we come to the end of our exploration into why trading is the best job, it's important to reflect on the profound journey this profession offers. Trading is not just about buying and selling; it's a way to transform your life. It challenges you, molds you, and ultimately empowers you to take charge of your financial future and personal development.

Throughout this book, we've delved into the **10 compelling reasons** that set trading apart as an extraordinary career choice. From the unlimited income potential to the invaluable lessons in self-discipline and emotional resilience, each reason highlights the unique opportunities that trading provides.

However, the journey doesn't stop here. Every trader's path is filled with ups and downs, victories and defeats. The real measure of success in trading lies not only in the profits earned but also in the lessons learned and the growth achieved along the way. Embrace each experience, for they shape your trading skills and your character.

Trading is a lifelong learning process. The markets are ever-changing, and adapting to these changes is what keeps the profession vibrant and engaging. Stay curious, remain open to new strategies, and continue to seek knowledge. The more you invest in your education, the more equipped you will be to navigate the complexities of the market.

As you embark on or continue your trading journey, remember that you have the power to create your own reality. The skills you develop and the mindset you cultivate will not only enhance your trading but also enrich every aspect of your life.

Thank you for joining me on this exploration of trading as the ultimate job. May you find the freedom, wealth, and personal growth that trading offers. Embrace the challenges, celebrate your successes, and never lose sight of the incredible potential that lies ahead. Your journey is just beginning, and the best is yet to come.

Welcome to the world of trading—where your future is truly in your hands.

AFTERWORD

As we conclude our journey through the compelling reasons why trading is the best job, it's essential to take a moment to appreciate the transformative potential this profession holds. Trading is not merely a means to an end; it is a profound experience that shapes our perspectives, challenges our assumptions, and empowers us to take control of our destinies.

Reflecting on the **10 reasons** outlined in this book, it becomes evident that trading offers more than just financial rewards. It provides an avenue for personal growth, resilience, and self-discovery. The lessons learned in the markets extend far beyond trading strategies and financial principles; they reach into the very core of who we are, teaching us about discipline, patience, and the importance of continuous learning.

For those who choose to embark on this path, remember that the journey will not always be straightforward. There will be hurdles to overcome, emotions to navigate, and times when doubt may creep in. Embrace these challenges as part of the process. Each obstacle is an opportunity to learn, adapt, and emerge stronger. The true essence of trading lies in your ability to evolve, both as a trader and as a person.

As you move forward, keep the spirit of exploration alive. The financial markets are dynamic, and staying informed and engaged will enhance your success. Surround yourself with a supportive community of traders, share your experiences, and learn from one another. The path to mastery is not a solitary one; collaboration and shared wisdom can provide invaluable insights.

Finally, let your passion for trading fuel your commitment to the craft. Whether you're trading full-time or as a side endeavor, approach each day with curiosity and dedication. Let the thrill of the markets inspire you, and never lose sight of your goals.

Thank you for taking the time to explore the profound world of trading. May your journey be filled with success, fulfillment, and the freedom that comes from being the architect of your own financial future. Remember, in the world of trading, the possibilities are limitless, and your potential is boundless.

Here's to your future as a trader—may it be as bright and rewarding as you envision.

AFTERWORD

Lorem ipsum dolor sit amet, consectetur adipiscing elit, sed do eiusmod tempor incididunt ut labore et dolore magna aliqua. Ut enim ad minim veniam, quis nostrud exercitation ullamco laboris.

AFTERWORD

ACKNOWLEDGEMENT

Writing this book has been a transformative journey, and I owe a heartfelt thank you to everyone who has supported and inspired me along the way.

First and foremost, I want to express my deepest gratitude to my mentors and teachers in the trading community. Your wisdom, guidance, and unwavering belief in my potential have shaped my understanding of trading and enriched my life in ways words cannot fully capture. Thank you for sharing your knowledge and experiences, which have laid the foundation for my success.

I extend my appreciation to my fellow traders who have walked alongside me on this path. Your camaraderie, support, and shared experiences have been invaluable. The countless discussions, late-night brainstorming sessions, and moments of encouragement have made this journey not only bearable but truly enjoyable. Together, we have celebrated our victories and learned from our challenges.

To my family and friends, thank you for your love and encouragement. Your belief in my vision kept me motivated during the times when the road seemed daunting. I am grateful for your understanding and support as I navigated the ups and downs of this profession.

I would also like to acknowledge the countless authors, thought leaders, and experts in the field of trading whose works have inspired me. Your books, articles, and teachings have not only deepened my knowledge but also ignited my passion for this profession.

Finally, thank you to the readers of this book. Your willingness to explore the world of trading and consider its possibilities means the world to me. I hope this book inspires you to embrace the challenges and rewards that trading offers and encourages you to pursue your own journey toward financial freedom and personal growth.

— GODFX

ABOUT THE AUTHOR

Godfx

GODFX is a highly successful trader and financial educator with over a decade of experience in the financial markets. With a background that spans various trading styles—including day trading, swing trading, and long-term investing—GODFX has developed a unique approach to navigating the complexities of the trading world.

Driven by a passion for helping others succeed, GODFX has dedicated much of their career to sharing valuable insights and lessons learned from both triumphs and setbacks. Through a combination of analytical rigor and psychological resilience, they have cultivated a reputation for understanding not just the mechanics of trading but also the mindset required for success.

Having faced the challenges and pitfalls that many traders encounter, GODFX understands the importance of mastering effective habits. Their commitment to continuous learning and personal growth has led to a wealth of knowledge that they are eager to share with aspiring traders.

As a sought-after speaker and mentor, GODFX has inspired countless individuals to adopt disciplined trading practices and cultivate the habits necessary for long-term success in the markets. This ebook is the culmination of years of experience, research, and reflection, aimed at providing readers with practical strategies to enhance their trading effectiveness.

When not trading or educating others, GODFX enjoys engaging with the trading community, exploring new market trends, and continuously refining their own trading strategies. They believe that trading is not just a profession but a lifelong journey of learning and self-discovery.

PRAISE FOR AUTHOR

GODFX is a true visionary in the world of trading. His deep knowledge, passion, and commitment to sharing his expertise have not only transformed his own life but continue to inspire countless others on their trading journeys.
— ANONYMOUS

A masterful guide! GODFX breaks down complex trading concepts into simple, actionable steps. His insights into building a legacy through trading are both profound and practical. This book is a must-read for anyone serious about financial freedom.
— ANONYMOUS

GODFX's approach to trading is as empowering as it is effective. He not only teaches how to succeed in the markets but how to grow as a person. This is more than a book about trading; it's about building a life of purpose.
—ANONYMOUS

Rarely do you find someone as dedicated to helping others achieve their potential in trading as GODFX. His passion for teaching and sharing his knowledge is evident in every chapter. This book will change the way you view trading.
—ANONYMOUS

BOOKS IN THIS SERIES

The Trading Matrix: Breaking The Code To Financial Freedom

Imagine a world where the financial markets are no longer a mystery, but a matrix of opportunities waiting to be unlocked. In The Trading Matrix, GODFX pulls back the curtain on the complex systems that drive market movements, revealing a hidden code that, when understood, can unlock the path to financial freedom. This groundbreaking guide breaks away from traditional trading books, offering a fresh perspective on the art and science of profitable trading. Whether you're a beginner or an experienced trader, this book will challenge everything you think you know about the markets and provide you with the strategies, tools, and mindset needed to decode the market's secrets and achieve consistent success. Are you ready to break free and master The Trading Matrix?

10 Habits Of Highly Effective Traders

Unlock Your Trading Potential with "10 Habits of Highly Effective Traders"!

Are you ready to elevate your trading game? In this essential guide, GODFX, a seasoned trader with over a decade of experience, reveals the ten crucial habits that distinguish successful traders from the rest. Drawing from personal experiences and hard-won lessons, this book provides practical strategies that can transform your trading approach and lead to lasting success.

What You'll Learn:·

Discipline and Consistency: Discover how maintaining a disciplined mindset can enhance your decision-making and help you stick to your trading plan, even in volatile markets.

Risk Management: Learn essential techniques for managing risk effectively, ensuring that you protect your capital while maximizing your potential returns.

Continuous Learning: Embrace the importance of lifelong learning in trading, including how to stay informed about market trends and improve your skills.

Emotional Resilience: Develop the psychological strength needed to navigate the emotional ups and downs of trading, allowing you to make sound decisions under pressure.

Adaptability: Understand the necessity of being flexible and adapting your strategies to the ever-changing market environment.

Whether you are a novice trader looking to build a solid foundation or an experienced trader seeking to refine your approach, "10 Habits of Highly Effective Traders" provides actionable insights that will empower you to reach new heights in your trading journey.

Join thousands of successful traders who have transformed their trading practices with these essential habits. Take the first step toward mastering the art of trading today!

Get your copy now and unlock the habits that lead to trading success!

10 Reasons Why Trading Is The Best Job

10 Reasons Why Trading Is The Best Job is your ultimate guide to understanding why trading is not just a profession, but a life-changing journey. In a world where conventional careers often lead to dissatisfaction and limitations, trading offers a unique opportunity for financial independence, personal growth, and unparalleled freedom.

In this inspiring book, you'll discover:

Unlimited Income Potential: Learn how trading can empower you to break free from traditional salary constraints and tap into a world of limitless earnings.

Flexibility and Independence: Explore how trading allows you to design your own schedule, work from anywhere, and truly take control of your life.

Constant Learning and Growth: Dive into the continuous learning journey that trading offers, helping you develop invaluable skills that extend far beyond the markets.

Personal Development: Understand how trading challenges you to confront your fears, build discipline, and cultivate resilience.

Impactful Wealth Creation: Discover how you can create meaningful wealth not only for yourself but also for your community.

This book is packed with practical insights, motivational stories, and actionable advice that will inspire both aspiring traders and seasoned professionals. Whether you're considering trading as a career or looking to deepen your existing knowledge, 10 Reasons Why Trading Is The Best Job will guide you on your path to success and fulfillment.

Unlock your potential and step into a world where the possibilities are endless. Transform your life through trading and discover why it truly is the best job you can have!

Perfect for:

Aspiring traders
Financial enthusiasts
Anyone seeking freedom and personal growth
Take the first step toward your trading journey today!

BOOKS BY THIS AUTHOR

10 Habits Of Highly Effective Traders

Unlock Your Trading Potential with "10 Habits of Highly Effective Traders"!

Are you ready to elevate your trading game? In this essential guide, GODFX, a seasoned trader with over a decade of experience, reveals the ten crucial habits that distinguish successful traders from the rest. Drawing from personal experiences and hard-won lessons, this book provides practical strategies that can transform your trading approach and lead to lasting success.

What You'll Learn:·

Discipline and Consistency: Discover how maintaining a disciplined mindset can enhance your decision-making and help you stick to your trading plan, even in volatile markets.

Risk Management: Learn essential techniques for managing risk effectively, ensuring that you protect your capital while maximizing your potential returns.

Continuous Learning: Embrace the importance of lifelong learning in trading, including how to stay informed about market trends and improve your skills.

Emotional Resilience: Develop the psychological strength needed to navigate the emotional ups and downs of trading, allowing you to make sound decisions under pressure.

Adaptability: Understand the necessity of being flexible and adapting your strategies to the ever-changing market environment.

Whether you are a novice trader looking to build a solid foundation or an experienced trader seeking to refine your approach, "10 Habits of Highly Effective Traders" provides actionable insights that will empower you to reach new heights in your trading journey.

Join thousands of successful traders who have transformed their trading practices with these essential habits. Take the first step toward mastering the art of trading today!

Get your copy now and unlock the habits that lead to trading success!

10 Reasons Why Trading Is The Best Job

10 Reasons Why Trading Is The Best Job is your ultimate guide to understanding why trading is not just a profession, but a life-changing journey. In a world where conventional careers often lead to dissatisfaction and limitations, trading offers a unique opportunity for financial independence, personal growth, and unparalleled freedom.

In this inspiring book, you'll discover:

Unlimited Income Potential: Learn how trading can empower you to break free from traditional salary constraints and tap into a world of limitless earnings.

Flexibility and Independence: Explore how trading allows you to design your own schedule, work from anywhere, and truly take control of your life.

Constant Learning and Growth: Dive into the continuous learning journey that trading offers, helping you develop invaluable skills that extend far beyond the markets.

Personal Development: Understand how trading challenges you to confront your fears, build discipline, and cultivate resilience.

Impactful Wealth Creation: Discover how you can create meaningful wealth not only for yourself but also for your community.

This book is packed with practical insights, motivational stories, and actionable advice that will inspire both aspiring traders and seasoned professionals. Whether you're considering trading as a career or looking to deepen your existing knowledge, 10 Reasons Why Trading Is The Best Job will guide you on your path to success and fulfillment.

Unlock your potential and step into a world where the possibilities are endless. Transform your life through trading and discover why it truly is the best job you can have!

Perfect for:

Aspiring traders
Financial enthusiasts
Anyone seeking freedom and personal growth
Take the first step toward your trading journey today!

www.ingramcontent.com/pod-product-compliance
Lightning Source LLC
Chambersburg PA
CBHW070349230526
45471CB00006B/2487